Fairground adventure

Nick Beare and Jeanette Greenwell

The fairground adventure................. page 2
The fairground adventure – questions ...... page 26
Funfair facts............................ page 28
Funfair facts – questions .... page 29
Great fairground rides .... page 30
Great fairground rides – questions .... page 31

The fairground adventure

Richard ran up to the ball. 'Are you ready, Jack?' he shouted.

'Ready,' shouted Jack.

Richard kicked the ball to his friend. His sister, Gail, watched them.

'Can I play too?' she asked.

Richard shook his head. 'Girls don't play football,' he said.

Gail didn't answer. She was angry with Richard. 'He is horrible sometimes,' she said to herself. 'Never mind, I'll go to the funfair.'

The fairground music was playing. It was happy music. Gail walked towards the fairground entrance. Then she stopped. She didn't want to go to the funfair alone. That was no fun. She looked at the two boys.

Jack saw her stop, and he ran towards her.

'Don't be angry, Gail,' he shouted. 'Wait for us. Then we can all go to the funfair.'

Richard kicked the ball one last time, but he kicked it too hard. The ball flew past Jack, over the entrance, and into the fairground.

'Oh no!' Jack shouted. 'Can you see it, Gail? Can you see the ball?'

'No,' said Gail. 'There are so many people. Wait! Yes, it's on the ground by the ice cream stall. I'll go and get it. Oh no!'

There was a man in a red jacket next to the ice cream stall. He saw the ball and picked it up. He looked at it, then he put it in his bag.

'Hey!' Gail shouted. 'That's our ball!'

The man didn't hear her. He walked away with the ball in his bag.

The three children stood at the fairground entrance.

'Come on,' said Jack. 'Let's go into the funfair and find the man.'

'There are hundreds of people,' said Richard. 'How are we going to find him?'

'He has a bag and he's wearing a red jacket,' said Gail. 'I remember that.'

They went to the ice cream stall.

'I can't see him,' said Jack.

'Look!' said Gail. 'Over there! That's him!'

The man in the red jacket was waiting next to the roller coaster.

'Come on,' said Richard, 'before he gets on it.'

They ran towards the roller coaster.

'Where is he?' asked Jack. 'I can't see him now.'

Gail pulled Jack's arm. 'He's over there,' she said very quietly. 'But what's he doing?'

'He's… He's… I think he's taking that lady's purse,' said Jack. 'Yes, he is. He's a pickpocket! Hey! Stop that!'

The man turned and looked at the three children, then he began to run.

'He's got your purse!' Gail shouted to the woman as they ran past her.

'He's going on the roller coaster!' said Richard.

The man ran past the entrance and jumped into one of the cars.

Richard jumped into the last car just in time. Gail and Jack followed him.

'I hate roller coasters!' screamed Richard.

'Hold on tight, then!' shouted Gail.

The roller coaster rushed down and then up. Everybody screamed, except Gail.

'Look, Richard!' she shouted. 'The people look like toy soldiers.'

'I can't look!' said Richard.

Down and up, the roller coaster rushed on...

Richard's eyes were shut. He opened them for a second.

'I can't believe this,' he said. 'It's horrible!'

He closed his eyes quickly as the roller coaster went down again.

'When is this going to stop?' said Jack. 'I think I'm going to be sick!'

The roller coaster went up again... up and up and up. They were at the top of an enormous drop! Gail loved the roller coaster, but she closed her eyes too, this time.

Woosh! Down they came.

The roller coaster slowed down as it came to the entrance. Gail opened her eyes quickly. She saw the man. 'He's getting off now,' she said. 'Come on.'

'I can't move,' said Richard, but Gail and Jack pulled him out of the car.

'We must follow him,' said Jack. 'He's got our ball, and that lady's purse.'

'He's going to the Ghost Train!' said Gail.

They ran to the Ghost Train. They jumped into the last car. The train began to move. The doors of the Ghost House opened, and the car went in.

Inside it was completely dark. The train went very fast. There was a flash of lightning, and a ghost jumped out at them. They all screamed this time. Then it went dark again.

'I hate this,' said Richard. 'I really, really hate this.'

'The man probably hates it too,' said Gail. 'But we must follow him.'

'Can you see the man?' asked Jack.

'He's in the first car. I can't see him,' said Gail, 'but there's a skeleton. Ooooh!'

A skeleton jumped out of the wall, and bats flew in front of them. The people on the Ghost Train shouted and screamed.

Richard closed his eyes. He wanted it to finish.

Suddenly Gail shouted in his ear. 'Richard! Jack is trying to get to the man!'

Richard opened his eyes. He saw Jack climbing into the next car.

'Jack! Don't do that!' Richard shouted. 'You're going to hurt yourself!'

They both saw Jack's head for a moment, then – nothing.

'Maybe he fell...' said Richard. 'Maybe he...'

'No, Richard, I'm sure he's all right,' said Gail. But she wasn't sure. She couldn't see Jack, and she was worried.

15

There were more flashes of lightning. They heard horrible laughter, and they saw huge spiders on the wall. Richard was very unhappy.

'Where are you, Jack?' he shouted. 'Where are you?'

The Ghost Train was very noisy. It was impossible to hear anything. It was very dark in the Ghost House. Five minutes was like an hour!

At last the Ghost Train went more slowly. It was nearly the end of the ride. They could see doors at the end of the track. The doors opened.

'It's finished!' said Gail.

Suddenly, there was light everywhere... and there was Jack in the second car! He was right behind the man!

'Where's our ball?' he shouted.

But the man jumped out of the first car and ran round a corner. The three children followed him.

Jack saw it first. 'The Hall of Mirrors! He's going to the Hall of Mirrors!'

'But it's closed!' said Richard. 'Look at the sign!'

18

Gail ran round to the back. The man wasn't there. She saw a door. It wasn't quite closed.

'That's the exit,' she thought. 'I'm sure the man is inside.' She pulled the door open and went inside. The door closed behind her.

Outside the Hall of Mirrors, the boys looked for Gail.

'I don't understand,' said Jack. 'Where's Gail? She's disappeared.'

Richard was very worried. 'This is all my fault,' he said. 'I lost the ball, and I was horrible to Gail. We must find her.'

They found the door at the back of the Hall of Mirrors. It wouldn't open.

'I'm sure she's in there,' said Richard. 'We must get help.'

Inside the Hall of Mirrors, it was very quiet. Gail walked along a dark passage.

'I liked the roller coaster,' she thought. 'And the Ghost Train didn't worry me. But I don't like it here. Where are the boys?'

At the end of the passage, there was another door.

'Here goes!' said Gail, and she pushed the door open.

Suddenly there was lots of light. Here it was – the Hall of Mirrors! Gail looked around. In the mirrors, she saw ten Gails. Then she saw ten men in red jackets in the mirrors too! They all looked angry. Gail was frightened. Which was the real man?

The man moved quickly and all his reflections moved too.

'He's trying to run away again,' thought Gail.

Then she heard a shout. 'Gail, where are you?'

It was Richard. Gail turned round and saw him, the real Richard. Jack was behind him, with a big policeman.

But the man in the red jacket looked in the mirrors and saw twenty boys and ten big policemen. He was very frightened.

'I'll come quietly,' he said.

The policeman took him outside. The children followed them.

'Thank you, that was good work!' the policeman said to the children, and he took the man away.

Gail ran after the policeman. 'He has our ball,' she said.

The man took the ball out of his bag and gave it to her. She ran back to Richard and Jack.

'Here's the ball,' she said.

'Thank you, Gail,' said Richard. 'I'm sorry I was horrible. Will you play with us?'

Gail smiled. 'Let's all have an ice cream first,' she said. 'Then I want another ride on the roller coaster!'

'Oh no!' said Richard, and they all laughed.

The fairground adventure – questions

1. What game were the boys playing outside the fairground?
2. Why was Gail angry with Richard?
3. Who picked up the ball in the fairground?
4. What was the man wearing?
5. What did the man take before he ran on to the roller coaster?
6. Who liked the roller coaster ride? Who didn't like it?
7. Where did the children see the skeleton?
8. What did Jack do on this ride?
9. Where did Gail disappear?
10. Why did the boys look for a policeman?
11. What made the man frightened?
12. What do you see in a mirror?
13. What did the man give to Gail?
14. What two things did Gail want to do in the end?

15 Where does this ride go? Look at the picture and write five sentences. Use one of the words in the box to help you with each sentence.

| over | through | round | between | under |

Funfair facts

Everyone loves the fun of the fair. There are lots of different things to do. You can test your strength with the big hammer, you can eat ice cream or candy floss, and you can go on roundabouts, swings, bumper cars, or other exciting rides.

All over the world there are fairgrounds and amusement parks. Many cities in the world have fairgrounds which are open all year round. In some countries, smaller travelling fairs visit a town or a village. The fair stays for a week or a few days. When it is finished, the fairground workers pack everything very carefully into lorries and move on to the next place. Then they put their rides and stalls up and start all over again. They look after the machines that drive the rides. They live and travel with the fair.

About a hundred years ago most fairground rides were driven by steam engines. You can still find some of these 'steam fairs' today, as the picture above shows. But in modern fairgrounds, the rides use electricity. On the next pages you can read about some of these rides.

Funfair facts – questions

1 Name three different things you can do in a fairground.

2 What is a 'steam fair'?

3 Which picture shows a big wheel ride?

4 What does a travelling fairground worker do?

5 How do modern fairground rides work?

Great fairground rides

The Corkscrew ride is on the Gold Coast in Australia. You can see the loops of the 'corkscrew' in the picture.

When you go round a loop in a roller coaster, you don't fall out of the car when it is upside down. Why is this?

Because the car is moving fast and in a circle, your body is pressed into the seat of the car, and away from the centre of the loop. Of course, you wear a safety harness as well.

The loops on this ride turn riders upside down three times, at speeds of 100 kilometres an hour!

The High Roller is the world's highest roller coaster. It is in Las Vegas, in the USA. The ride runs 300 metres above the ground, around a huge tower, called the Stratosphere. The cars carry you round the top of the Stratosphere three times.

If you keep your eyes open, you can see the city of Las Vegas below you, as the next picture shows.

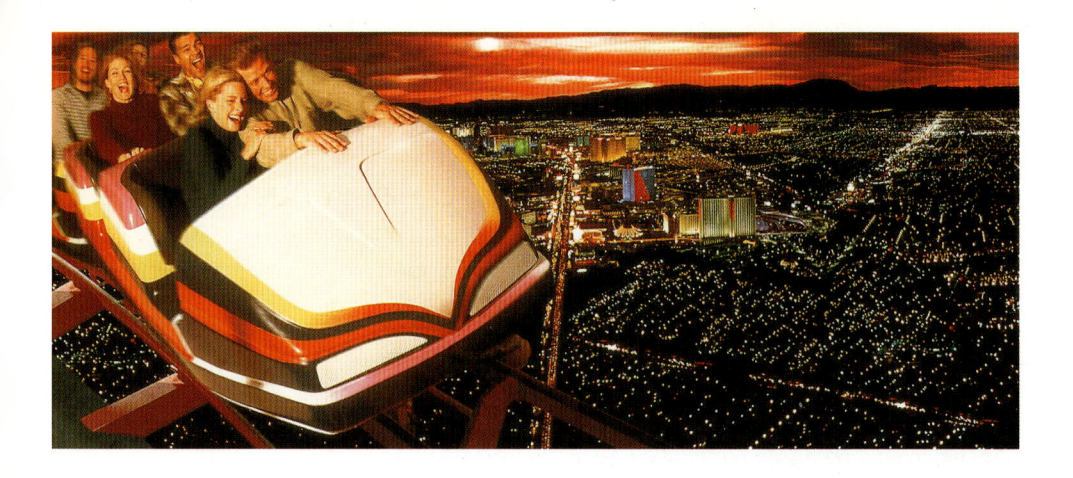

The other Stratosphere ride, the Big Shot, sends its riders up the tower in two seconds. These two rides use enough electricity to supply a small town!

Great fairground rides – questions

1 In which country can you find the Corkscrew ride?

2 How many times are its riders turned upside down?

3 Why is the Stratosphere ride called the High Roller?

4 Do the Stratosphere rides use a lot of electricity, or a small amount?

5 This picture shows a bumper car ride. What happens on this ride?

31

© Copyright text Nick Beare and Jeanette Greenwell 1998
© Copyright illustrations Macmillan Education Ltd 1998

The author asserts his moral rights.

All rights reserved. No reproduction, copy or transmission of this publication may be made without written permission.

No paragraph of this publication may be reproduced, copied or transmitted save with written permission or in accordance with the provisions of the Copyright, Designs and Patents Act 1988, or under the terms of any licence permitting limited copying issued by the Copyright Licensing Agency, 90 Tottenham Court Road, London W1P 9HE.

Any person who does any unauthorised act in relation to this publication may be liable to criminal prosecution and civil claims for damages.

First published 1998 by
MACMILLAN EDUCATION LTD
London and Oxford
Companies and representatives throughout the world

ISBN 0-333-67498-7

10 9 8 7 6 5 4
07 06 05 04 03 02 01 00

This book is printed on paper suitable for recycling and made from fully managed and sustained forest sources.

Printed in Egypt by Zamzam Presses.

A catalogue record for this book is available from the British Library.

Acknowledgements
The authors and publishers wish to acknowledge, with thanks, the following photographic sources: Robert Harding Picture Library pp28; 29. Tony Stone Worldwide p30 (photograph Robin Smith). Stratosphere Tower, Las Vegas p31 above. TRIP p31 below (photograph Heléne Rogers)

Illustrations by Annabel Spenceley/John Martin and Artists

The publishers have made every effort to trace the copyright holders, but if they have inadvertently overlooked any, they will be pleased to make the necessary arrangements at the first opportunity.